HOMEMADE PERFUME

Create Exquisite, Naturally Smell for You and Everyone

Copyright © 2020

All rights reserved.

DEDICATION

The author and publisher have provided this e-book to you for your personal use only. You may not make this e-book publicly available in any way. Copyright infringement is against the law. If you believe the copy of this e-book you are reading infringes on the author's copyright, please notify the publisher at: https://us.macmillan.com/piracy

Contents

How To Make Your Own Perfume At Home 1

A DIY Solid Perfume Trio 3

Jasmine Aloe Perfume Body Spray 7

Sandalwood Vanilla Solid Perfume 9

DIY Perfume Recipe Using Essential Oils 12

DIY Perfume Recipe Using Flowers 14

DIY Citrus Perfume Recipe 16

DIY Natural Vanilla Perfume Recipe 20

Solid Perfume Using Coconut Oil 22

DIY Patchouli Perfume Recipe 24

DIY Summer Perfume Recipe 26

Perfume Locket 28

DIY Fruit Roll-On Perfume Recipe 36

Perfume Bottles 40

Flower Oil Perfume 44

Peppermint And Grapefruit Perfume Recipe 47

Natural Perfume Oils 49

How To Make Your Own Perfume At Home

Every woman needs a signature scent that's utterly and recognizably her own. The best perfumes work with your body chemistry, and just a whiff of it can be a magical thing. If you're feeling crafty and creative, make your own scent. You can use exciting scents and ingredients from the convenience store to make your very own toxic-free, signature perfume right at home. These DIY perfume recipes are one of the easiest DIY projects and also make for a super unique homemade gift idea!

Before you learn how to make perfume at home, here's what you need to know about the basics of perfume notes. They're separated into three classes:

1. **Top Notes:** Top notes represent the first impression of your fragrance. They're generally the lightest of all notes, and fade the quickest. The most common ones include citrus, herbs, and light fruits like berries.

2. **Middle Notes**: The 'heart of your perfume', or the middle notes, make an appearance once your top notes evaporate. They last longer and have a strong influence on the base notes to come. The heart could be anything from rose to lavender, and geranium to lemongrass.

3. **Base Notes:** The final fragrance notes that appear once your top notes are completely evaporated are the base notes. These mingle with the middle notes to create the full body of your scent. These are often rich notes and linger for hours. Common base notes include vanilla, musk, cedarwood, patchouli and so on.

A DIY Solid Perfume Trio

This DIY solid perfume trio uses essential oils to create custom fragrance blends with aromatherapy benefits. It's perfect for giving as a gift!

HOMEMADE PERFUME

Prep Time	Cooling Time	Total Time
10 mins	3 hrs	3 hrs 10 mins

Course: DIY Beauty
Keyword: essential oils, holiday gifts, perfume   Yield: 6 tins
Author: Stephanie Pollard   Cost: $15

Equipment

- Microwave safe bowl
- 2-ounce metal tins with lids

Materials

- 4 tablespoons beeswax
- 5 tablespoons almond oil
- Essential oils

Instructions

1. Calming Blend

- 4 tablespoons beeswax
- 5 tablespoons almond oil
- 20 drops bergamot
- 15 drops vanilla
- 20 drops patchouli
- 2 ounce metal tin with lid.

Combine beeswax and almond oil in a small bowl. Microwave in 30-second intervals until melted. Add your essential oils and stir to combine, then pour into a lidded tin and let cool.

2. Energizing Blend

- 4 tablespoons beeswax
- 5 tablespoons almond oil
- 25 drops grapefruit
- 10 drops ginger
- 20 drops lemongrass
- 2 ounce metal tin with lid

Combine beeswax and almond oil in a small bowl. Microwave in 30-second intervals until melted. Add your essential oils and stir to combine, then pour into a lidded tin and let cool.

3. Joyful Blend

- 4 tablespoons beeswax
- 5 tablespoons almond oil
- 18 drops bergamot

- 15 drops orange
- 20 drops geranium
- 10 drops lemon
- 2 ounce metal tin with lid

Combine beeswax and almond oil in a small bowl. Microwave in 30-second intervals until melted. Add your essential oils and stir to combine, then pour into a lidded tin and let cool

Jasmine Aloe Perfume Body Spray

Inspired by the desire for a light summer fragrance, this perfume body spray is gently moisturizing, with an intoxicating scent. Like all things in summer should be, this recipe is super simple. To streamline ingredients and save you a step, we used a witch hazel infused with aloe vera. Unlike other alcohol-based body mists, the witch hazel will lock in moisture without drying skin, while aloe vera provides hydration without any greasy residue. For a vanity-worthy twist, we filled the spray with dried flowers and large mica flakes, however you can opt out if you choose.

HOMEMADE PERFUME

Materials

- 3 oz witch hazel with aloe vera
- 1 oz vegetable glycerin
- 25 drops of jasmine essential oil
- assorted dried flowers
- flaked mica optional

Instructions

1. Fill 4 oz spray bottle with dried flowers and mica, if using.
2. Add witch hazel and glycerin.
3. Top with 25 drops of jasmine essential - adjust if you'd like it stronger.

Sandalwood Vanilla Solid Perfume

Materials

1. 1 teaspoon almond oil
2. 1 ½ teaspoons shea butter
3. 1 teaspoon beeswax pastilles or shavings
4. 20-25 drops sandalwood oil diluted in a carrier oil, or more for a stronger scent
5. 30-35 drops vanilla oil diluted in a carrier, or more for a stronger scent

Instructions

1. Begin by adding the almond oil, shea butter and beeswax to a double boiler. If you don't have one, you can make do by filling a saucepan with several inches of water and placing a heat safe bowl on top. Try to use a bowl that has a pour spout so you can easily transfer your perfume to the containers (like a glass liquid measuring cup).

2. Bring the water in the saucepan to a simmer and slowly melt your almond oil + shea butter + beeswax combination over a medium heat. When they are completely melted, pull the bowl off the heat, add the sandalwood and vanilla oils, and mix thoroughly.

3. Now it's time pour your mixture into your containers. Fill them up to the top with the melted perfume then allow them to harden completely. It doesn't take long! Once they're finished, toss one in

your purse to use on the go. These lovelies will stay good for 8-9 months and make for great gifts!

Note: This recipe uses sandalwood and vanilla oils that have been already diluted in jojoba oil. If you would like to substitute another blend of essential oils that are more pure, be sure to adjust the amount you use accordingly.

DIY Perfume Recipe Using Essential Oils

What You Need

- 2 tablespoons carrier oil (grapeseed, jojoba, sweet almond or anything of your preference)
- 6 tablespoons of vodka (100 proof vodka)
- 2.5 tablespoons bottled water
- 30 drops of essential oil (9 for your top notes, 15 for your middle notes, and 6 for your base notes)

- A small funnel
- Coffee filter
- 2 clean dark glass bottles with airtight lids

How To Make Perfume Using Essential Oils

1. Pour your preferred carrier oil into one of the glass bottles. Add your base, then middle, and then the top notes.
2. Add the alcohol.
3. Secure the lid, and let your perfume sit for a solid 48 hours. (Remember, while making perfume with essential oils, the longer you let it sit, the stronger the scent, so you can leave it for up to 6 weeks if you wish.)
4. Once you're satisfied with the strength of the scent, add the water, and shake the bottle vigorously for 1 minute.
5. Use your filter and funnel to transfer the scent to the other bottle.

DIY Perfume Recipe Using Flowers

What You Need

- 1 1/2 cups chopped flowers
- Medium-sized bowl with lid
- 2 cups distilled water
- Cheesecloth
- A small saucepan
- Washed and sterilized, small glass bottle with an airtight stopper

How To Make Your Own Perfume With Flowers

1. Start by gently washing your flower petals, removing any dirt with water.
2. Soak the flowers overnight in a cheesecloth-lined bowl and cover it with a lid.
3. Squeeze the pouch of flowers over a saucepan, extract the flower-scented water and simmer over low heat until you are left with about a teaspoon of the liquid.
4. Pour cold water into this liquid and bottle it up.
5. Leave it to set overnight!

DIY Citrus Perfume Recipe

What You Need

- 1 tablespoon jojoba oil
- 30 drops of essential oils – grapefruit, sweet orange, peppermint, and a chamomile/lavender blend
- 2 tablespoons of vodka
- 1 tablespoon distilled water
- Dark glass container
- Small glass container
- Glass perfume bottle

Steps

1. Add jojoba oil to the glass container and then add alcohol.
2. For your essential oils, follow this order: base note: 10 drops of grapefruit, middle note: 10 drops of sweet orange, and then 5 drops of peppermint, top note: 5 drops of chamomile/lavender blend or just lavender.
3. Use a dropper to add distilled water.
4. Mix these ingredients well and transfer to a glass container. Let this sit for 48 hours or longer, as per your preference.
5. Transfer to a perfume bottle once it has reached the desired scent.

DIY Jasmine Perfume

What You Need

- 2 tablespoons vodka
- 1 tablespoon distilled water or orange blossom water
- Essential oils – 30 drops of jasmine, 5 drops lavender, and 5 drops of vanilla
- Glass bottle
- Cheesecloth

Steps

1. Mix your essential oil blend with the vodka in a glass bottle.
2. Leave the mixture to sit for two days.
3. Add distilled water or orange blossom water to the mix and shake gently.
4. Leave for about four weeks in a cool, dark spot.
5. If you see any sediment, strain through a cheesecloth and pour the perfume in a spray bottle.

DIY Natural Vanilla Perfume Recipe

What You Need

- 1 vanilla bean
- 3 to 4 tablespoons organic sunflower oil
- 40 drops of bergamot essential oil
- Cedarwood and anise essential oil
- Glass containers

Steps

1. Start by slicing open a vanilla bean, scrape out the seeds from the pod, and cut them up nicely into tiny pieces.
2. Place these pieces in a glass bottle and add your organic sunflower oil.
3. Close your bottle tightly and let it sit in a cool, dark place for two weeks (shake the bottle gently once every 3-4 days.)
4. After two weeks, add bergamot, cedarwood, and anise essential oil to a glass spray bottle.
5. Use a dropper to get the vanilla infused oil out without getting the seeds.
6. Add this to your glass spray bottle and finally, gently shake the blends together.

Solid Perfume Using Coconut Oil

What You Need

- 2 tablespoons beeswax
- 2 tablespoons fractionated coconut oil
- 20 drops of your favorite essential oil

Steps

1. Add fractionated coconut oil and beeswax to a glass jar.
2. Place the jar in a saucepan with about 2 inches of boiling water.
3. Stir ingredients until combined.
4. Once it has melted, remove from heat and let it rest for 3-4 minutes.

5. Add your essential oil and stir well.
6. Pour this into a container, and to use, apply a small amount to your skin.

DIY Patchouli Perfume Recipe

What You Need

- 2 tablespoons vodka
- 1 tablespoon distilled water
- A dark glass bottle
- Essential oils – 20 drops sweet orange oil, 10 drops patchouli oil, 10 drops cedarwood oil, 5 drops of lavender oil, 5 drops of ylang-ylang oil, 5 drops bergamot oil

Steps

1. Start by combining your alcohol and distilled water into the dark glass bottle.

2. Add a drop of your essential oil, stir that drop into the mixture (the idea is to stir each drop slowly into the alcohol, so the oils thoroughly disperse in it.)
3. Once you finish, let it sit for about two days.
4. Gently shake before you use!

DIY Summer Perfume Recipe

DIY   Summer   Perfume   Recipe   -   DIY   Perfume

What You Need

- 13 drops peppermint essential oil
- 13 drops rosemary oil
- 5 drops lemon essential oil
- 5 drops sage essential oil
- 3 tablespoons vodka
- 2 cups distilled water

Steps

1. Mix all your essential oils in a glass bottle that contains your 100 proof alcohol.
2. Gently shake and let the bottle sit for about two days.
3. Add the distilled water, mixing slowly until it's completely dispersed.
4. Leave your perfume to sit for 2-3 weeks in a cool, dark place.
5. After your perfume matures, remove any kind of sediment using a filter and store it in a pretty glass spray bottle.

Perfume Locket

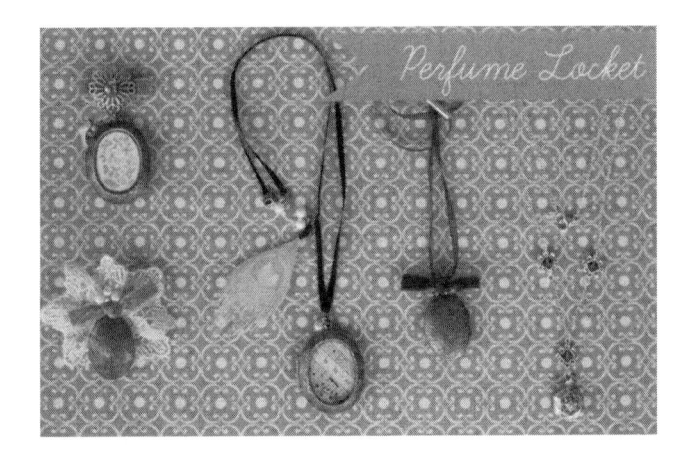

My inspiration comes from an adorable perfume locket I found at Anthropologie a few months ago. It's such a great idea for today's bride (or bridesmaids!) who have limited purse/pocket space, and this project does double duty as a functional accessory that is pretty and will keep you smelling lovely at the same time. I just knew it would be the perfect DIY project for any bride looking to have something unique and eye catching, and that can even be amended for a groom or groomsmen. Just use an empty pocket watch casing instead of a locket, and work it into a boutonniere with some manly smelling essential oils. I've included the solid perfume how to, and some photos of different style of lockets to get your creativity jumpstarted! Happy crafting!

Materials (will make 5-7 lockets, depending on size):

- 2 tbsp Beeswax
- 2 tbsp Olive Oil, Sweet Almond Oil, or Jojoba OilEssential oils (Some great scents are Jasmine, Lavender, Vanilla, Ylang ylang, Citrus, etc. You can find these at natural food stores, craft stores or online)
- Clean, empty jar
- Wooden skewer or clean straw
- Empty locket

Making the perfume:

Step 1: Using a cutting board and a knife (preferably items that you don't mind getting waxy) cut one of the beeswax blocks into shavings. I ordered my beeswax from Honeyrun Farms, an Etsy shop that sells their homegrown honey, beeswax, soaps and candles. One of their 1 oz blocks equals about two tablespoons of beeswax.

Step 2: Once the beeswax is in thin shavings, put it into the jar with the olive oil. Place the jar into a sauce pot with about an inch or two of water in it, and heat on medium to low until the mixture is completely melted.

Step 3: Use the skewer or straw to stir and help break up the beeswax until it is smooth. Take off of heat.

Step 4: Measure out 20-40 drops of essential oils. I did this beforehand into a small dish so that I could immediately pour it into the wax/oil mixture without it having a chance to set up. Since I did a Lavender Vanilla scent, I used about 15 drops of Pure Vanilla Extract (yes, the kind you use for baking! Imitation vanilla will not substitute here) and 20 of Lavender essential oil. Stir well into the mixture.

Step 5: Once the scents are mixed into the beeswax mixture, very carefully begin to pour into the lockets. I wrapped a towel around the jar since the wax was still really hot. Fill the lockets up to the edge of the hollow part, being careful not to overfill. If it gets into the part with the latch, it's okay, the clasp will still lock since it is a soft wax. Fill both sides if you want, or leave one side open for a photo.

Step 6: Let the perfume solid sit for about 30 minutes. It should be dry to the touch, and you can just swipe your finger across and apply!

You may find that throughout the process of making the perfume that you stop smelling the scent you've put in. Don't worry, your nose has just adapted to it. You will be able to smell it after being away from it for an hour or so.

Suggested Jewelry Materials:

- Lockets
- Ribbon, chain, lace
- Pin backs
- Beads, charms, crystals
- Findings (clasps, jump rings, eye pins)
- Assorted jewelry tools (pliers, round nose and flat, wire cutters)

For the jewelry, assemble the materials you will need for your lockets. Think of what you want to make: a necklace, bracelets, brooches, something to pin to your bouquet, etc. I find that sketching out some ideas first helps a lot, then you can know exactly what materials you need, and you have a sort of blueprint to follow as you assemble your jewelry.

Also consider the style of your wedding. Do you have a lot of vintage elements? You might want to find lockets with a nice patina, paired with lace and some vintage glass beads. Do you love classic style, a la Audrey Hepburn? Go black and white with some white peacock feathers and pearls. Are you giving these as gifts to your bridesmaids, or mother of the bride? Make each one different, perhaps adding a small charm that represents something about the woman you are making it for.

Choose lockets that are a bit larger to get the best results. Small lockets will work, but they will not hold much perfume. I'd suggest keeping the size to about an inch or larger. Have fun scouring antique stores and flea markets or even Ebay for vintage lockets and findings. This will be more expensive though, so check local craft stores for supplies as well. I found my lockets at Michael's and Joann's and paid an average of $4 per locket. You will also need a good pair of wire cutters, round nose and flat nose pliers. You can buy a jewelry tool kit at craft stores for about $15, or just raid your fiance, boyfriend, husband or dad's toolbox!

DIY Fruit Roll-On Perfume Recipe

What You Need

- A 5 ml roll-on bottle
- 3 drops mandarin essential oil
- 2 drops sweet orange essential oil
- 3 drops neroli essential oil
- 2 drops cedarwood atlas essential oil
- 1 teaspoon liquid carrier oil (grapeseed oil or fractionated coconut oil)

Steps

1. Start by dropping your essential oils into a bottle and gently swirl around to mix.
2. Add your carrier oil.
3. Transfer this to a roller bottle.
4. Put the lid on and roll between your hands to mix.
5. Roll onto your wrists and behind your ears to use.

DIY Rose Perfume Recipe

What You Need

- 3/4 cup fresh rose petals
- 1/2 cup 100 proof vodka
- 2 1/2 cups distilled water
- 2-3 drops rose essential oil
- Big glass jar with a lid
- Glass perfume bottle

Steps

1. Start by placing your rose petals at the bottom of your glass jar and pour the vodka over it.
2. Cover this up and let it sit for a day in a cool, dark place.
3. Use a spoon to squish the petals and add the distilled water into the jar as well as the drops of essential oil.
4. Cover the bowl and leave it to sit for 5-7 days, making sure you mix it once a day.
5. Once this concoction has been sitting for a week, strain this mixture into a glass perfume bottle. Shake well, and it's ready to use!

Perfume Bottles

Materials:

- Glass bottles
- Assorted crystal beads
- Bead pins and caps
- Needle-Nose Pliers
- Glass paint (optional)

Step One: Make the bottle topper

Thread a bead pin through the hole of a teardrop crystal bead and loop it a couple of times, pulling tightly to hold in place. If the bead is round then thread a bead cap onto it before adding the bead.

Step Two: Attach the bottle topper

Remove the cork from the glass bottle and position a bead cap on top of the cork. Push a pin all the way through the center to create a hole in the cork. Thread the bead pin through the hole and twist the end tightly to hold the bead topper in place.

Step Three: Embellish with glass paint

Add embellishments to the bottle using glass paint. You can create any type of design, but I found that lines of dots made a lovely texture and were easy to draw.

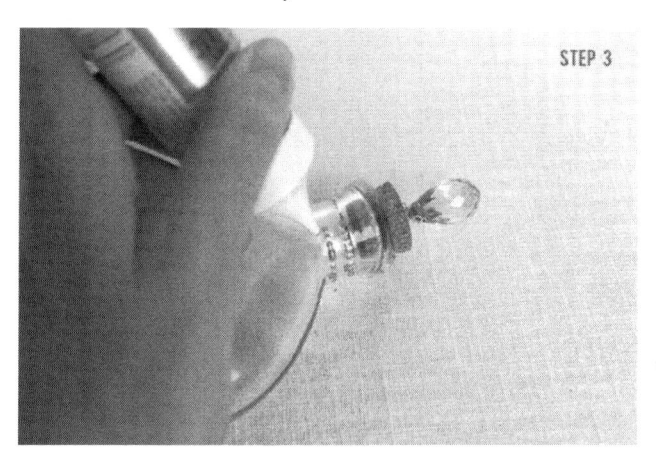

Step Four: Fill with a handmade perfume or any other liquid of your choice.

HOMEMADE PERFUME

Flower Oil Perfume

Ingredients:

- Mason Jar/ any glass jar with a lid
- Two-three flowers like a Rose or Arabian Jasmine (Mogra)
- Unscented oil (olive oil, sunflower oil, almond oil, jojoba oil or coconut oil)
- Spoon, strainer
- A spray bottle or small glass/plastic container to store the perfume
- Jasmine Flower Oil

Procedure:

1. Pluck the petals of the flower, ensure that the petals do not have water droplets on them. You can dry out the flower by keeping it under a fan for 10-15 minutes. Do not dry the petals in sunlight.
2. Take around 5 tablespoons of oil. You can adjust the quantity of oil based on the number of flowers you are taking. You need only as much oil, as is necessary to soak the petals.
3. Heat up the oil to lukewarm and put it inside the glass jar
4. Now, put all the petals inside the glass jar. Press the petals gently, so they get submerged in the oil
5. Close the lid, and keep the jar in a warm room for 24 hours.

6. Next day, open the lid and strain out the petals from the oil.
7. Your perfume is ready!
8. Collect the oil in the small glass container and apply it as perfume

If you want this perfume to smell stronger, then add a fresh batch of moisture-free petals of the same flower to the oil collected in step 6 and repeat the whole process. You don't need to heat up the oil collected in step 6.

Peppermint And Grapefruit Perfume Recipe

What You Need

- A small glass container
- Dark glass container to store
- Glass perfume spray bottle
- 1 tablespoon jojoba oil
- 2 tablespoons pure grain vodka or alcohol

- 30 drops of essential oils – grapefruit, peppermint, sweet orange, and a chamomile/lavender blend
- 1 tablespoon distilled water

Steps

1. Add the jojoba oil to the glass container and then add your alcohol.
2. Add the essential oils in the following order: base note – 10 drops of grapefruit, middle note – 10 drops of sweet orange and 5 drops of peppermint, top note – 5 drops of chamomile/lavender blend.
3. Use a dropper to add distilled water.
4. Mix this well and transfer to a dark glass container. Store this for two days or up to six weeks.
5. Transfer your perfume to a pretty glass spray bottle once it reaches your desired scent.

Natural Perfume Oils

CALMING CREAMSICLE

- 16 drops Vanilla in Jojoba Oil – Base note
- 8 drops Roman Chamomile Essential Oil – Middle note
- 16 drops Sweet Orange Essential Oil – Top note
- Equal parts Sweet Almond Oil and Apricot Seed Oil – Carrier oils
- Flower petals like dried rose buds, dried yellow hibiscus, or purple petals. These are purely ornamental so don't worry about their scent.

BEARDED BAE FRAGRANCE

- 48 drops Lime Essential Oil – Top note
- 24 drops Bergamot Essential Oil – Middle note
- 48 drops Sandalwood Essential Oil Blend – Base note
- Equal parts Sweet Almond Oil and Apricot Seed Oil – Carrier oils
- Flower petals

We put Calming Creamsicle into a 10 ml roll-on bottle, but if you have a larger 30 ml roll-on bottle then multiply those amounts by 3, or follow the formula below.

DIRECTIONS

- Step 1 – Add your base note into the bottle, the base note should always go in first.
- Step 2 – Add your middle note into the bottle. Swirl the bottle to mix.
- Step 3 – Add your top note. Swirl the bottle to mix these three together.

- Step 4 – Smell your mixture, and at this point you can tweak the scent to your liking by adding drops where you see fit.
- Step 5 – Fill the rest of the bottle to the top with equal parts of the carrier oils, we used sweet almond and apricot seed. Put the top on and shake until well mixed.
- Step 6 – Add in dried flower petals until it looks just right, and then pop on the roller ball and lid.

It's really easy, makes a beautiful gift, and you can flex your creativity with your scents and names. I'm going to try my own mix of orange oil (top note), jasmine oil (middle note) and amber oil (base note) because they're my favorites.

Printed in Great Britain
by Amazon